Surviving th
Organism and Dealing with
Problem Generators

The Life and Corporate Survival Guide

Surviving the Unnatural Organism and Dealing with Problem Generators

The Life and Corporate Survival Guide

Mark Camilleri

A catalogue record for this book is available from
the National Library of New Zealand.

ISBN 978-0-473-46297-0

Book production DIYPublishing.co.nz

Contents

Introduction

Twenty years ago, I was fast approaching forty years of age. I was sitting in a cheap wine bar with a few friends, and we were pondering why our lives hadn't really turned out the way we thought they would. Why did we all continue to have money problems? Why was our work not interesting? Why were we always stressed out? Why did we struggle in relationships, both professionally and personally (a few divorces here and there)? And by the more philosophical: Why are we here? What is my purpose? What's this thing called life all about?

Everyone among this group of friends had read many if not hundreds of feel-good/positive-thinking books, and yet we all still wondered why we didn't get to attract what we deserved or wanted. Even worse, I had seen some family and friends in the extreme being inflicted with the symptoms of boredom, apathy and materialism, which unfortunately led to alcoholism, drug addiction, depression, and, unfortunately in some cases, suicide. As we continued to drink (maybe too much), we all had a sense of dismay and confusion.

The problem of disillusionment had started at a young age. We were all unanimous in being brought up and conditioned to think that people are generally kind by nature, and that by reciprocating kindness to others, the world should be a better place. Once again, we all agreed that it appears that it's not like that – the pub talk enters the profound and the existential. We talked about the extremes where the human race has murdered or killed over a 100 million of its own kind in the last century alone in the name of God, or the fact that less than ten percent of the world's population controls over ninety percent of the world's wealth. Political goodwill or trust has become an oxymoron. We were conditioned by our ancestors to the concepts of hard work and goal setting, only to find out that nothing of substance had really materialised.

Now, on to the personal level: when I first started these memoirs aged forty and hair greying, I figured I should have been more prosperous and happier by then. It took me a long time and meeting up with wiser folks and some really good fortune to finally work out what the problem was, and more importantly, what the solution might be. It took me at least ten years past my fortieth birthday to hit an epiphany, the secret sauce of breakthroughs (so to speak), and I have made many mistakes along the way. Now, thanks to some dogged persistence by mentors and friends, I can finally put pen to paper.

So, what is the solution? First, let's start by referring to the problem as a 'disease', and like a lot of diseases, if left untouched it can be extremely contagious and dangerous.

Fortunately, I was not alone in discovering the cause and effect of the problem that is referred to as the Problem Generator (PG) affliction. During one of my stints as managing director of a Silicon Valley software company, I was introduced to the nuances of PG affliction by Brian Connors of Monet Executive Solutions.

Brian was a business problem solver, who started me on the journey of corporate effectiveness and efficiency. By analysing the layers of my work activity Brian was able to demonstrate to me how this PG disease was a major cause of managerial inefficiency in the workplace. Working side-by-side with me, Brian had witnessed that I had been wasting ninety percent of my time on dealing with problem generators, which was both counter-productive and stressful to others and me in the workplace.

Over the years, I believe I have further refined these basic concepts what Brian had taught me, and I also believe that I have expanded the ideals and principles of PG prevention for general use in one's life by fundamentally demonstrating that the disease can be treated both by prescriptive and preventative measures.

The main objective of this book is to establish a usable guide on how to eradicate PGs from your life for good!

The first part of this book refers to the definition, concept and awareness of problem generators. The second part is designed to help you build an internal radar to help you eradicate PGs from your life, or at least mitigate their influence in order for you to be free and unhindered in your goal to feel inner peace, and to have true joy in achieving your goals.

This book is primarily aimed towards helping those people entering corporate life for the first time or for those long-timers who have been disillusioned in their careers. I hope to achieve this by focusing on the source of the problems and not the symptoms, i.e. the myths surrounding perception and reality about corporations and relationships. Whilst my reference and examples have been taken from the corporate world, I believe these 'golden nuggets' can be applied equally to all facets of life in general.

1

Problem Generators: The Behavioural Contagion

The solution to the disease of problem generators will become evident later on in the book. The first task here is for all of us to wake up to the modern epidemic referred to as the Problem Generator affliction.

We see the PG affliction and its consequences every day when it causes mayhem and disturbance to one's life to the point where dreams and goals are forever being reassessed, postponed, frustrated or simply put in the 'too hard basket'. Moreover, and may the gods help us if this happens to be our 'best case' scenario, we have been told we can overcome all forms negativity in the presence of PGs by simply reading the abundance of positive, feel-good literary works by authors like Chopra, Tolle, Dyer, Gawain, Grabhorn and so on. However, PGs seem to have also read those books, which unfortunately blunts the message of hope and optimism from those authors mentioned above. Trust me, PGs will consume you mentally, and sometimes physically, one hundred percent of the time. It is so hard to be positive when PGs surround you. It is even more difficult to identify and label these PGs, especially when a systemic method or approach has not been published to date.

2

Problem Generators: The Background

PGs are growing in numbers at an alarming rate in our society. The reasons for this proliferation are varied and many. However, here is my list of observed behavioural traits of PGs:

- obsessive materialism and greed

- lack of communication

- inability to delay gratification

- lack of spiritualism

- egoism

- victim mentality (somebody else needs to take the blame for all my problems)

- social welfare dependency

- lack of mentors

- managing and parenting by fear

- sensationalistic media hype

- lack of self-esteem

- desensitisation to violence and crime

- the excessive need to conform to societies' norms (to be liked regardless of principles).

These are but a few of the main causes. On a macro level, we see the excessive desire or greed of egocentric minds within government administrations and corporations who continually use false news and messaging in order to deceive its population and employees to obtain their goals. A typical and well-worn tactic, for example, is government deception to persuade its citizens that war can be based on just grounds – the so-called 'domino effect' of communism (Vietnam), or 'evil' military juntas (Mandela's ANC), or suppressive dictatorships (Cuba) or by invading and killing people in countries who 'possess' weapons of mass destruction (Iraq). As I have mentioned before, humans have killed over 100 million human beings during the last century by using this deceptive, ego-based method in trying to convince society that something is seriously wrong with us if we don't trust the 'spin'! This is why most people who are consciously aware believe that we have totally lost the plot and that the human species as a whole can be rightly justified as being insane. If we are to have any chance of surviving as compassionate, peaceful, loving beings, we must remedy our education system, or at least supplement our citizens' knowledge at an early age with this insight into PG behaviour, and facilitate PG removal by a systemic process of non-violent interactions and early warning detection methods to avoid any initial introduction of PGs into our world.

As I said earlier, this worldwide condition is spreading like an out-of-control cancer. In fact, what makes it so uncontrollable is that this 'disease' is not restricted to age, race, religion, socio-economic group or political persuasion. It is totally non-discriminatory. So, unless we become aware (even partially) of the true conscious behaviour of our 'being-ness' (i.e. the state of non-ego, non-attachment and non-separateness), then we will continue to suffer, particularly in the hands of PGs.

From my point of view, enjoyment of life begins when we prevent PGs from entering our life in the first place in order to clear the decks and get on to what we truly deserve. Simply put, this book takes us on a journey where we are the scriptwriter and director of our own creativity. Once we remove ourselves from the attachment of form and material possessions, life, paradoxically, becomes more abundant. Life goes with the flow that you create. However, if we don't understand why and how PGs entered our lives in the first place, then we will continue to attract and experience the same depressing results and feelings every day. If enough people are taught how to handle PGs, then I sincerely believe the true domino effect of human nature will be everlasting joy and freedom throughout society.

However, dealing with problem generators is only the beginning of this life-changing process. You must, in parallel (to removing PGs), get to a place where you have replaced the negative energy that first caused the attraction of PGs into your life with a process that deliberately puts you on a footing of creating your *own* (not someone else's) desired dreams and happiness. Life abhors a vacuum; therefore, in my experience, it is important to work on both processes at the same time. These processes are creative visualisation *and* PG elimination. Once you 'clear the decks' (PG elimination), you must immediately replace it with what you want in order to fill the vacuum (creative visualisation).

For example, if you are presently at loggerheads with a highly troublesome neighbour, simply moving to another suburb will not solve the problem, particularly if you have not learnt the lessons that attracted the problem neighbour to you in the first place – did you treat the neighbour with disdain or prejudice? Did you prejudge the neighbour on a particular day (maybe it was at the height of the conflict when emotions were running high)? Did you make judgement calls based on assumptions? Are you creating a toxic environment based on jealousy or envy? In other words, are you bringing negative energy to the scene? Every time you sense the release of a negative thought or word, flipping your 'switch' to a positive creative mode will help you attract the right creative energy to your environment. PGs detest a creative, positive environment and will less likely be attracted to your world of joy and positiveness. So, by using creative visualisation techniques, you can establish an environment for growth and solution development. This is difficult to achieve when surrounded by negative thoughts and negative people.

The most common ego identifications have to do with possessions, the work you do, social status and recognition, knowledge and education, physical appearance, special abilities, relationships, person and family history, belief systems, and often nationalistic, racial, religious, and other collective identifications. None of these is you. —*Eckhart Tolle*[1]

Similarly, when dealing with bad relationships, do you consistently move on to a new partner with the hope that the grass will be greener on the other side? Moving on to another relationship may not necessarily resolve the problem if the issues surrounding the departure or the reasons why you attracted such a person into your life the first place were not resolved within yourself; the grass may be greener on the other side of the mountain, but everyone has to mow the lawn eventually.

Furthermore, if you do not understand the true reasons why such an attraction occurred, then I can assure you that another PG, or, more debilitating, the PG within yourself, will continue to repeat the same scenario over and over again. History will repeat itself until your lessons are learnt.

The same may be said of your job. If performance targets (KPIs;

---

1 Goodreads. (2018). *Eckhart Tolle quotes*. Retrieved from https://www.goodreads. com/author/quotes/4493.Eckhart_Tolle?page=3.

Key Performance Indicators) are consistently not being met or you have encountered troublesome work colleagues, then moving to another company or complaining about your high quotas may not necessarily be the answer until you have become aware and understood the law of attraction.

This concept is not new. Hundreds of books have been written on the subject; however, the problem lies in the consistency of a practical approach that needs to be applied on a daily basis. The law of attraction simply understands the Biblical notion of reaping what you sow. The challenge lies with the fact that most people do not know how to deal with their problems or, worse still, they become so dominated or related to their problems that it becomes entrenched as their present life situation – as Tolle puts it, you become associated with your 'pain body' and you become reluctant to let it go: 'Even if blame seems more than justified, as long as you blame others, you will keep feeding the pain body with your thoughts and remain trapped in your ego. There is only one perpetrator of evil on the planet: human unconsciousness. That realisation is true forgiveness. With forgiveness, your victim identity dissolves, and your true power emerges—the power of Presence. Instead of blaming the darkness, you bring in the light.'[2]

This feeding of your pain body then spirals into a feeling of uncontrollability, which ultimately leads to frustration and despair. However to overcome this state of unease, the technique of creative visualisation will help rectify this situation, as author Shakti Gawain states:[3]

Creative visualization is the technique of using your imagination to create what you want in your life. There is nothing at all new, strange, or unusual about creative visualization. You are already using it every day, every minute, in fact. It is your natural

2   Tolle, E. (2016). *A new Earth: Awakening to your life's purpose.* New York, USA: Penguin Books.

3   Gawain, S. (2002). *Creative visualization: Use the power of your imagination to create what you want in your life.* Novato, CA: Nataraj Publishing.

power of imagination, the basic creative energy of the universe, which you use constantly, whether or not you are aware of it.

Four Basic Steps for Effective Creative Visualization:

1. Set your goal

Decide on something you would like to have, work toward, realize, or create. It can be on any level – a job, a house, a relationship, a change in yourself, increased prosperity, a happier state of mind, improved health, beauty, a better physical condition, solving a problem in your family or community, or whatever.

At first, choose goals that are fairly easy for you to believe in, that you feel are possible to realize in the fairly near future. That way you won't have to deal with too much negative resistance in yourself, and you can maximize your feelings of success as you are learning creative visualization. Later, when you have more practice, you can take on more difficult or challenging problems and issues.

2. Create a clear idea or picture

Create an idea, a mental picture, or a feeling of the object or situation exactly as you want it. You should think of it in the present tense as already existing the way you want it to be. Imagine yourself in the situation, as you desire it, now. Include as many details as you can.

You may wish to make an actual physical picture of it as well, by making a treasure map (described in detail later). This is an optional step, not at all necessary, but often helpful (and fun!).

3. Focus on it often

Bring your idea or mental picture to mind often, both in quiet meditation periods, and also casually throughout the day, when you happen to think of it. In this way it becomes an integrated part of your life, and it becomes more of a reality for you.

Focus on it clearly, yet in a light, relaxed way. It's important not to feel like you are striving too hard for it or putting an excessive amount of energy into it – that tends to hinder rather than help.

4. Give it positive energy

As you focus on your goal, think about it in a positive, encouraging way. Make strong positive statements to yourself: that it exists; that it has come or is now coming to you. See yourself receiving or achieving it. These positive statements are called "affirmations." While you use affirmations, try to temporarily suspend any doubts or disbelief you may have, at least for the moment, and practice getting the feeling that what you desire is very real and possible.

Continue to work with this process until you achieve your goal, or no longer have the desire to do so. Remember that goals often change before they are realized, which is a perfectly natural part of the human process of change and growth. So don't try to prolong it any longer than you have energy for it — if you lose interest it may mean that it's time for a new look at what you want.

If you find that a goal has changed for you, be sure to acknowledge that to yourself. Get clear in your mind the fact that you are no longer focusing on your previous goal. End the cycle of the old, and begin the cycle of the new. This helps you avoid getting confused, or feeling that you've "failed" when you have simply changed.

When you achieve a goal, be sure to acknowledge consciously to yourself that it has been completed. Often we achieve things that we have been desiring and visualizing, and we forget to even notice that we have succeeded! So give yourself some appreciation and a pat on the back, and be sure to thank the universe for fulfilling your requests.

To use creative visualization it is not necessary to believe in any metaphysical or spiritual ideas, though you must be willing to entertain certain concepts as being possible. It is not necessary to "have faith" in any power outside yourself.

The only thing necessary is that you have the desire to enrich your knowledge and experience, and an open enough mind to try something new in a positive spirit.'

Hence the need to work on both processes – creative visualisation *and* PG elimination.

Remember, you are what you attract. You are not separated from the whole. You don't get in life what you deserve; you get what you negotiate through your passion, feelings and energy on a consistent, daily basis. Until you believe that you are the sole creator of your outcomes, your life will be run by chance and circumstance. In other words, your life will be out of control or, worse, in the hands of PGs. This is often the precursor to emotional fear and subsequent anxiety or depression.

As stated previously but worth repeating: problem generators' debilitating behaviour can and will (if not dealt with) destroy your passion, kill your dreams, shatter your self-confidence and prevent you from achieving your right to experience the joys of life. Hence, the objective of this book is to live our lives not in fear but in joy and inner peace. Most sages throughout time have stated that motivation or action that is based on *love* is the most rewarding because it draws you to your real purpose in life. On the contrary, motivation or action that is *fear*-based will often leave you empty, even if good results are sporadically achieved. This is because the intrinsic feeling of fear is not removed from its foundations. It is important to note that fear is bestowed mainly upon us by PGs. In fact, if you allow fear to be your source of energy, then anxiety and worry will be your constant companions. This often leads to desperate, ruthless, underhand and depressive behaviour that usually results in destructive outcomes by eventually trying to win at all costs. And this ultimately leads to your emotional downfall, which is unfortunately exacerbated by hurting those around you (who are usually the ones that love you the most). It often leaves you (if you have a conscience) with the feeling that you have sold your 'soul to the devil' – worthless and empty. Your true purpose in life is never found because you have not let your true self and desires step forward and reveal themselves; rather, you have allowed the external conditions of worry and fear control your actions and feelings. Life then becomes a perpetual hell. We need to break these habits of fear-based dream stealers and become creators of life manifestation even if it appears not to be the 'right or comfortable' thing to do at the time. The main point is to be patient and to have faith as we are trying to remove years and years of fear-based conditioning (which, by the way, is the DNA of the corporate style of management).

I will repeat this several times, as it is at this point where most people give up, especially when money (debt), fear and greed are involved. Please don't forget that it is often said that the biggest sin on earth is not the fact of having your less-than-perfect, moral body buried when you die, but having your unfulfilled dreams buried along with it. As Emerson writes:

The mass of men worry themselves into nameless graves while here and there a great unselfish soul forgets himself into immortality.[4]

Is it simple to achieve this level of awareness? Hell no. However, once you have mastered this technique, in a very short period of time your life will change forever. Remember, you cannot get new results with old repeatable habits. So, let's permanently change those habits that continually produce rotten results.

To quote Lynn Grabhorn: 'Like any hidden talent that you've either consciously or unconsciously known was there but didn't

---

4   McAlary, B. (28 Jan, 2013). *Legacy* [blog]. Retrieved from http://
    slowyourhome.com/legacy/

feel comfortable bringing out, once you accept the fact that wanting is part of you, and that doing it is really okay, it becomes fun. Joy starts to flow. You begin to vibrate differently, for when you are in joy with Life you cannot vibrate negatively and you cannot attract negatively, only positively.'[5] Simply put, what happens on the *inside* controls the *outside*. People and things *will* enter your life based on the level and type of energy you percolate through your life. Life will move in direct proportion to the amount of energy you are 'vibrating' and feeling.

This is precisely why I have based the book on the law of attraction as the main vehicle to obtain true purpose of life. Have you ever seen a person who is truly 'on purpose' with their life? Things just seem to flow with ease and they look so serene and happy in doing what they do.

So, how can you lead a life of high-level positive feelings when your present reality is laced with confusion, people problems (PGs) and financial burdens?

This, in my view, has been the hardest chasm to cross and has not been adequately addressed in all those positive-thinking books written over the last twenty or so years.

However, I do wish recognise two excellent books: Lynn Grabhorn's work, *Excuse Me, Your Life is Waiting*, and Eckhart Tolle's masterpiece, *The Power of Now*. These works have formed the basis of what Clarence Smithison eloquently states is 'the ability to see the invisible – to believe in the incredible which enables you to receive what masses think is impossible.'[6]

Difficult to believe, highly sceptical and far-fetched! I thought so too. However, if you are in doubt about your need to change, then simply ask yourself, 'Have my actions over the last five years

---

5   Grabhorn, L. (2015). *Excuse me, your life is waiting: The astonishing power of feelings.* (Expanded study edition.). Charlottesville, HA: Hampton Roads Publishing Company, Inc.

6   The-Modern-Christian.com. (2007–2013). *Christian quotes.* Retrieved from http://www.the-modern-christian.com/christian-quotes-1.html

got me to where I wanted to be today?' And, 'If I keep on doing the same thing for the next five years, am I going to be any closer to my dreams or goals?' If the answers are no, then continue reading.

I believe that once you have practiced and had fun with the basic ingredients of creating happiness and joy through your own efforts, then the next step is to arm yourself with a pragmatic toolkit that you can use to clear your environment of internal and external problem generators. The aim here is for you to be self-sufficient, and to *quickly* prepare and create the environment for success you so richly deserve. The hard but not impossible task is to detach from the destructive social conditioning and misguided individuals who wish to impose their ill-directed motives and aims against you. However, please be reminded that these people tend to direct this unconscious behaviour towards you because they simply 'do not know what they do'.

I have been teaching the subject of wealth creation and problem generation for over twenty-five years now. I enjoy teaching mainly because I learn more about myself every time there is interaction with the students, but more importantly, I like to keep track of the results that others have obtained.

The results achieved within the last five years of seriously applying this technique have been nothing short of startling. Results: No more money problems, less stress, the unbelievable situation of being in a worry-free condition *all* the time, enhanced self-confidence, and the increased ability to set and achieve new and higher goals and to improve relationships on all levels. I repeat, I am now completely free of debt and I have helped many others achieve this freedom. By freeing yourself from debt you become conscientiously aware of your true inner self and realise that the negative aspects of fearing debt hid the many capabilities you have within, like feeling and thinking of the right choices to make precisely at the right moment in time, which are not based or clouded by judgement or fear. This paradigm will paradoxically enable you to achieve your goals of financial freedom or goals of obtaining better relationships. From my own experience and also from teaching others, by not fearing or being overly absorbed by debt you become less bitter or manipulative in your dealings with individuals. You become less absorbed to make a 'buck' or to complete a transaction at all costs. You start focusing on relationships that enhance your joy or happiness within, which will enable the law of attraction to work its wonders. Hence all my present dealings and relationships with plumbers, gardeners, accountants, lawyers, real estate agents, financial planners, etc., are based primarily on trust and integrity. If these two elements are missing from the relationship, I will not engage with that person no matter how good the price or the deal might be!

Other results of the technique are that dreams and daily happiness that were once thought impossible or unattainable are now deemed a natural state of affairs. Relationships become obtainable and go from strength to strength. Finally, another wonderful by-product of practising the law of attraction is that physical health will improve because you will now be attracted to people who genuinely wish to foster well-being – both mentally and physically. You will notice more invitations will come your way to participate in events, and not just for the sake of making money but also in life itself! Your daily life will become more physically active. Positive people, you will observe, are into all aspects of life. Also, positive people are not 'couch potatoes' or mental inhibitors; you will notice a common trait where this group does not dwell in the past nor fear the future, which allows them to live in the present.

For sales people, targets and quotas will be achieved and/ or exceeded. Permanent smiles will form to the point where they will wonder what all the fuss was about in the first place and start thinking that maybe a conspiracy theory does exist to make us underperform and live life in constant stress and fear for the benefit or profit of others.

Yes, it appears unbelievable and cosmic, but, hell, who am I to argue if it works?

As stated earlier, this book is based on a foundation of Lynn Grabhorn's excellent book *Excuse Me, Your Life is Waiting* and the spiritual bible of the twenty-first century, *The Power of Now* by Eckhart Tolle. These works assume you are not a victim and that you take full responsibility for your actions and outcomes in your life.

Brian Connors deserves special mention again here. He has been my mentor and dear friend from Australia for many years and the one who has singularly lead me on to the path of dealing with PGs with his teachings.

Building on this foundation, I have delivered a practical approach to be used immediately, which, if applied daily, will guarantee you dramatic results within a short period of time. The body of this work was written over a three-year period so that 'real-life' case studies can be put to the test in 'real time'. However, like most 'new' things, you must have patience (even for you 'instant coffee' folk), persistence and faith. After all, I am trying to overcome years of social and parental conditioning in this wee book. Just remember what J.S. Mill once said,

No great improvements in the lot of mankind are possible, until a great change takes place in the fundamental constitution of their modes of thought.[7]

So, let us begin.

PGs can be found anywhere: in the family home, in the work place, shopping malls, in governments and in schools. In fact, as stated earlier, you may be your own worst problem generator. 'I think, therefore I am,' said Descartes. He found that he could not

---

7   Goodreads. (2018). *John Stuart Mill quotes*. Retrieved from https://www.goodreads.com/author/quotes/57651.John_Stuart_Mill

doubt that he himself existed, as he was the one doing the doubting in the first place. To extrapolate further from this observation, one may also conclude 'I am what I think'. If you have thoughts of negativity towards people or organisations, or simply believe that society owes you a living, you will become your own PG and you will suffer similar consequences. I have witnessed many friends and colleagues, trapped by their own egos and prejudices, produce systemic negative outcomes as a self-fulfilling prophecy. The internal PG within your mind (ego) seeks to blame everyone else but yourself (governments, employers, foreigners, neighbours, etc.) for goals not being achieved. The focal point of this frustration is established in your own mind and is accentuated by your own ego which continually seeks retribution for life's shortcoming by digging deeper and deeper into the cause of the problem. However, the 'problem' is one of your own generation; you created the negative thought, you continued with the negative thought and you attracted (maybe inadvertently) other negative people because your thoughts. Hence you have become your own problem generator!

3

Identifying Problem Generators

It is amazing how many of us have allowed enormous amounts of negative and destructive energy from PGs to enter our lives. They have an uncanny knack of transferring guilt and getting you to accept their problems and their warped version of reality. They are dream stealers. They suck oxygen out of life. They make you believe (falsely) that you are the problem. PGs are so good at transferring guilt and problems to the unsuspecting that we start to question our sanity. They are so good at what they do because they firmly believe their view is correct. As I said previously, it's a disease. And we have unfortunately allowed PGs to place us into untenable situations where we are left dwelling in the past and fearing the future with the unpleasant and soul-destroying feeling of missing the present.

Furthermore, PGs don't go away easily and will on average steal ninety-eight percent of your time and mental energy at any given moment – if *you* let them. They invariably achieve pleasure in running their lives and others' like daily soap operas such as Australia's *Neighbours or Home and Away,* or by adopting the life-styles of socially irresponsible glamour magazines like *Cleo* or *Cosmopolitan.*

OK, that's a little harsh. But let me clarify. If soaps and/or glamour magazines are used as a form of escapism or harmless entertainment, then that is fine; I have no problem with that. However, what I do object to is when someone lives out their life and those of others' like soap operas or with the belief that the content of these magazines that promote extreme concepts of win/lose, sad/happy, good/evil, deceit/honesty, pacifism/ violence, martyrdom/greed, beautiful/ugly, fat/thin, etc., are *true* reflections of a prosperous and joyous life. We have unfortunately developed a new damaging dialogue in our society called 'sitcom clichés'.

An example of this is a woman I once lived with who was quite attractive. 'Sharon' would purchase these lifestyle magazines in huge quantities; she would cut out pictures of 'attractive' thin models and soap opera stars, which were obviously electronically touched up by sophisticated computer enhancers. She then started to hang them up in the bathroom, inside her wardrobe, on the car's sun visor, kitchen cupboards, and finally on the back of the toilet doors. I also noticed over time that Sharon would paraphrase soap opera quotes both in normal conversation mode and also in the heat of an argument. She had become so obsessed with what she allowed society to condition her with, that she not only became a PG for others by literally becoming the quintessential 'drama queen', but sadly and more importantly, she had created an empty void within herself that lead to a poor self-image by believing that life must be perfectly lead in accordance with the images of her screen idols or graphic artists. Her life had become obsessed with celluloid 'reality'. Style was more important than substance. However, all through this she was, deep down, not happy. Unfortunately, at the time I was also a young, naive, unconscious incompetent in dealing with the issues of PGs. I could not help her. However, I feel that what I know now would have helped her and maybe it could have saved the relationship. Unfortunately, it was not meant to be.

Another example of a PG was a fellow employee at a company based in Australia where I was once managing director. On reflection and with hindsight, the early warning signs were always there. However, once again my ignorance and/or naivety failed to pick up the tell-tale signs (covered next chapter) of early PG behaviour. In the beginning, I had the pleasure and enjoyment of a good working relationship with 'Bridget' until I realised she was resting on her laurels, or, to use a colloquial term, she was bludging. She was given credit (and commission) on a deal that was part of a team effort that had closed well and truly over a year before. Unfortunately, she was given undue credit (this was my fault) for the deal because the account simply fell into her territory. After a period of time, she would come in late and not work or contribute in generating any further business for the company. In summary, she was loafing. This, from my point of view, was both unethical and unfair to the rest of the team. After many discussions with her about her lack of performance and with no improvement in sight, I placed her on medium-term objectives to get her to refocus on the targets which had not been met now for over twelve months. She responded, much to my amazement, with a vitriolic email attack against my directive. The email was like a nuked explosion. It was sent to all of the senior members of the company: the US founder and CEO, the human resources director, the global services consulting director, the international sales and marketing director and many others at senior level. However, this in it itself was not the source of my annoyance. It was the three-page email that had listed me, the economy, the weather, the local politics and so on for all the reasons (excuses) for her poor performance. I would later learn that this type of behaviour is nothing new for a PG and is often used to ensure blame is passed on to others instead of taking ownership and responsibility for themselves. What identified this particular person as a true PG, was the vitriolic attack on a personal level – the words 'abuse', 'favouritism', 'harassment', 'unfair', 'not my fault', 'under duress' and 'disappointed' were all repeatedly used in her emails. The old me would have sprung defensively like a leopard feverishly clawing through every scurrilous paragraph in her email and taken it apart one by one, word by word, with fact and substance. That was the 'old me'. The 'new me' deliberately refused to respond for twenty-four hours (the old adage 'sleep on it' applies here). There was too much emotion in the air. And as my mentor, Brian Connors, had advised me: by fighting heated emotion with fiery emotion, I would achieve only one possible outcome – a *negative* one. Therefore, the next day, with a clearer head and after much contemplation, I responded to her three-page attack by simply replying in an email with the sentence: Will you or won't you achieve the targets you agreed to at the beginning of the year by 30 June? (The year had only four months left to run. No results had been achieved to date for the previous nine months).

Bridget resigned the next day.

Brian Connors had taught me something special that day: a simple and effective technique in how to deal with PGs is to simply reply and transfer the issue back to the source. An individual who is a true PG always loves to play in the emotional cesspit of life. This is what they exist for. They want you to own the problem – even if the problem was of their creation. Hence, the key ingredient in dealing with this PG in this instance was to first defuse the situation by delaying the response, and, second, by replying in a simple, minimalistic and rational manner.

So, in summary, when dealing with PGs, keep the following in mind:

- Rise above the emotion (walk away and 'sleep on it').

- Do not defend the irrational or the absurd.

- Do not reply with a 'tit for tat' response. This will only condone the PG's behaviour and set the emotions into a spin; they will come back for more (it's in their DNA).

- Reply with fact and clearly outline the objectives which were agreed to in the first place.

- Do not compromise this approach. PGs see compromise as weakness or as 'giving in'.

- Your goal is for the PG to own their 'problem', *not* you!

In retrospect, I would have loved to identify all potential PGs before I allowed them to enter my inner circle (either through employment or friendships) in the first place. Yes, life is wonderful with hindsight. However, after twenty-five years of dealing with PGs, I have complied a simple checklist that will help:

Problem Generator Identifying Checklist

Look out for those individuals who:

- display or demonstrate a 'violin' or 'wooden leg' mentality

- tend to put others down in order to build themselves up

- appear indispensable or irreplaceable to others (which is nonsense)

- like to transfer guilt to others – it is never the PG's fault

- speak in negative terms about anything and everything in general (listen carefully and you will notice a pattern of negativity that may tend to be playful or in jest – it is not)

- display a scarcity mentality, i.e. never having enough of anything (money, love, material possessions, titles, recognition, etc.)

- appear to never be grateful or compliment others for anything

- always be wanting more and blaming others for not getting it

- appear as 'drama queens' with no empathy for others

- tend to plagiarise sentences from soap operas or popular sitcoms to get their point across

- create a mystery about themselves and their potential by talking in riddles, which creates an illusion of self-importance, but in reality, there is no substance

- tend to get emotional and irrational very quickly when confronted with fact (which is always the opposing view of the PG, who tends to deal in fake news)

- tend to bully and attempt to force their opinions as the only one that matters in the discussion

- always blame – a PG is never wrong, so it must be someone or something else's fault

- tend to get close to you whilst holding private agendas (which unfortunately the unwary find out too late – the damage is already done)

- tend to use emotional blackmail (the worst kind) to get their own way

- tend to be totally unreasonable and follow no logic

- tend to occupy 98% of your thoughts (in a bad way) and become 98% of your present problems.

In addition to these factors, PGs tend to be very lazy and always view themselves as victims, believing it is always someone else causing their predicament. For this reason, laziness must also be mitigated in all forms from your daily activities. This is fertile ground for PGs (including yourself). You cannot attempt to reach the euphoric state of happiness by being with someone or doing something that you simply have no desire to continue with, or to allow certain people to enter your world that you simply do not like. Remember that idleness creates a vacuum for a fertile vessel like a PG to enter. Find your life's purpose and approach it full-on with passion and energy. Try to achieve the goals you want by approaching it like a fully committed soldier, i.e. not in a half-hearted or 'half-pregnant' manner, but with an unconditional, fully committed behaviour that comprises good and positive thoughts, words and action tasks. Don't waste your time on anything else. Remember the paradox that money will flow to positive, energetic and purposeful people.

I have also found that people such as academics, professionals or analytically minded people often display more subtle PG signs. They are 'smart' PGs. I have found among this group a condition referred to as 'analysis paralysis'. For example, a close friend of mine, a doctor, had attended more self-development and self-help courses and clairvoyants than what I have had hot dinners in order to receive the 'answers' to life. He was annoyed that they didn't tell him how to live or what to do with his life. He continued to blame past teachers and clairvoyants as he sought out new ones. Though the good doctor had read every new self-help book that hit Amazon.com, he was confused and despondent as he failed to achieve happiness in his life. His goals were never achieved (and he often blamed the economy or someone else). As I write this, he is still looking for the panacea or magic pill to life. His training and upbringing lead him to believe that life must be lived rationally and logically – there must be winners and losers, or the answers must be black or white. However, in reality he was living a life based on circumstance and conditioning imposed by his peers. The good doctor had inadvertently become his own problem generator by delegating the right to create his own life to those around him.

I have also come to the conclusion that happiness is not dependent upon your environment. It is the state of mind one enters into when one diligently and persistently focuses on true loves and desires *unconditionally*. Discipline is required here so you are not unduly influenced by family and peers but rather through your desire to 'run your own race' on your terms, not set by those close or near to you. You run the risk of adopting their life scripts and goals that may or may not be what you want. It is also harder to deal with identifying or rectifying problem generator issues if you are following someone else's script rather than your own.

So, take your partners, sport, hobbies, family, spiritual awareness, work, and so on. Work through each area and focus on how you feel about what you have in your life. If the warm, tingling sensation or fuzzes are not felt with this exercise, then find out why by drilling down to the answer with meditation. Any form of meditation will suffice, even if you are a novice. Try and lie quietly for 20 minutes and listen to your inner self.

- Happiness is not in having or being, it's in the doing. The essence of true wisdom is to know that rest is rust, and that real life is activity, laughter and love.

- Your greatest success and happiness in life will be found when you use your natural abilities to their fullest extent.

- You were created to conquer your environment, to solve problems and to achieve goals.

- You'll find no real satisfaction or happiness in life without obstacles to conquer and goals to achieve.

- Yes, there is true happiness. It's found in doing a job well done, in achieving a worthy goal, in putting your children to sleep, and in writing the last line of your poem.

- Your personal growth itself contains the seed of happiness.

—Author Unknown[8]

---

8   Kreze, F. (28 Jan, 2016). *You will find true joy using your potential* [blog]. Retrieved from http://www.lmicanada.ca/blog/you-will-find-true-joy-using-your-potential.aspx

4

Money as a Problem Generator

If you wish to know your past life, look at your present
circumstances. If you wish to know of your future life,
look to your present actions. —*Buddhist saying*

First, let us get the often misunderstood, worrisome and paradoxical concept of money out of the way. Money is not, nor has it ever been, the issue or the problem here. However, if you don't get your life into balance and put the concept of money into perspective, financial wealth will at best evade you or at least bring immense emptiness and unhappiness into your life.

Why do you think the nominated all-time favourite movie among the wealthy is Olsen Welles' great epic *Citizen Kane*? Or why Andy Warhol's saying, 'In the future, everyone will be world famous for 15 minutes,'[9] ended up leaving him empty and destitute for most of his life? The fear of emptiness and solitude portrayed by these people is one they try to avoid.

Our goal should be to achieve a coordinated mix of a healthy mind, family, society, body and finances.

Money has attracted many unwarranted and misguided interpretations from parents and readers of the Bible like: 'money doesn't grow on trees', 'money doesn't buy love', 'save your money', 'money is the root of all evil' (the correct interpretation

---

9   Wikipedia. (2018). *15 minutes of fame*. Retrieved from https://en.wikipedia. org/wiki/15_minutes_of_fame

is, in fact, 'the *lust* of money is the root of all evil'), 'you will get money if you work hard', 'you need money to make money', and so on. No wonder, with this malignant image and self-defeating perception of money, that many of us are struggling financially. We have been continually conditioned to focus on the pending debilitating consequences (i.e. fear) of what both the lack of money and the abundance of money would bring to our lives. No wonder only ten percent of the population has ninety percent of the world's wealth.

Let's get down to the basics of money. As a visual, tangible item, it is neither sexy nor attractive. In fact, in some countries, like the United States, the look and feel of money is simply plain ugly (the greenback). Therefore, putting your energy towards money on its own merits won't work because the physical presence of money lacks passion or vision of desire.

Worrying about not having or having a big bank balance of 'Scrooge' proportions in your cheque account won't do it for you either, simply because you have not attached the correct emotions towards your wants or desires.

You are probably asking for and expecting repelling vibrations that attract poor outcomes. And if you do happen to fluke a jackpot, you will eventually see it blown away over time. The reason is not that most people don't understand the value of money. On the contrary, it is the value of the want associated with one's purpose that most people miss out on. We have been exorcised out of our dreams at an early age and told to get 'real'. The majority of us are living a reality based on *other* people's scripts, not our own.

So, you must flow your energy towards the uplifting feeling of what money can give you in the form of desires towards a purpose, otherwise money *won't* happen.

I cringe when I hear statements like: 'When I have enough money, I can really start to enjoy life'. Don't put the cart before the horse: This is the true paradox of the established belief of money.

If you truly and passionately desire a material or spiritual want, then the universe *will* provide the necessary means. The form will materialise, providing that your desire is consistently and persistently felt by your inner being.

So, chase your dreams and desires to the fullest extent of your passion. Use visualisation techniques – cut out pictures, hang them around the house, talk to them, feel the feeling of the items already in your possession and, if necessary, 'fake it until you make it'. This doesn't imply that you go into debt to 'fake it'. Rather, it is a mind game of visualising abundance (as opposed to scarcity) and, where necessary, preparing yourself or laying the framework for success with money, e.g. opening an online share brokerage account, opening with just $1 a trust account for the kids, getting daily updates of property trends, conversing with successful people, etc.

I am deliberately focusing on passion and consistency as two 'must haves' in your toolkit. Wishful thinking is just plain waffle. This is why 99.9% of New Year's resolutions fade away before January ends. The desire must be strong and felt in the pit of your stomach. To put my spin on Maslow's hierarchical needs theory from his book *Motivation and Personality*: the highest level of human self-actualisation is that *feeling* is the ultimate form of two-way intimate communication with the world. This is why I also love the *Celestine Prophecy* series by James Redfield, which reveals that following your intuition brings the universe into line with your destiny. Not the other way around.[10] This is a great story where 'wishing' thoughts 'need not apply'; however, 'passionate feeling' thoughts bring life into harmony.

In summary, going after money per se is a waste of time. Going after your dreams and aspirations is not. The name of the game is to remove money as an end game objective and to *drill* down on your *whys*. Why and how do you feel the way you do when you

---

10 Redfield, J. (2016). *Celestine Vision*. Retrieved from https://www.celestinevision.com/the-12-celestine-insights/

talk or think about your desires?

For example, a close friend of mine, Jenny, came to our house one day and we got talking about her dreams. I asked her what she wanted, and she stated that she wanted a new house. Jenny's delivery was flat with half a smile.

I replied, 'Why do you want a new house?'

'It provides security,' came her reply. Still no emotion. Actually, there was more concern in her voice than excitement.

I continued. 'How does that make you feel?'

With a full smile, Jenny said, 'Safe and independent.'

I carried on. 'How does it really make you feel to be safe and independent?'

She stood up with excitement and put her fist up like a true Scot, and said, 'It gives me the bloody feeling of freedom.'

Fantastic. Now we were at the right place of heart-felt vibration. I quickly replied, 'Trap that thought, bottle it, store it and never forget that "Brave Heart-feeling" of your "why".'

In this case, the 'why' was freedom.

It is so important to go beyond just positive thinking. Jenny was positive that she wanted a new house; however, she had not felt why she really wanted a new house or how she could afford it. She could not constantly tap into that feeling of desire because the feeling was one of lack, not of abundance. This is why most positive-thinking people fail to obtain their wants. This type of positive thinking is superficial or just plain veneer that is easily peeled away like the outer skin of an orange. They *think positively* but *act and feel negatively*. This is because they really have not drilled down into their true 'whys'.

I know this concept of obtaining money is hard to accept, but if you have trouble switching your thoughts away from money issues, then, once again, try 'faking it until you make it'. As Mihaly Csikszentmihalyi stated in his excellent book *Flow*: 'To overcome the anxieties and depressions of contemporary life, individuals must become *independent* of the social environment to the degree that they no longer respond exclusively in terms of it rewards and punishments.'[11]

Enjoy and have fun with this concept and treat it as a game. For example, I constantly look at my life cycle plan (sometimes up to five times a day), which is simply a cardboard poster that has photographs and cut-outs from magazines of all the things I truly desire: a BMW, a ski lodge, family bonding, skiing in France, two dogs, a helicopter, scuba diving in the Mediterranean and a house by the sea in Australia. Now, if you think that the desires of this author are OK for him because he has the money, or you may be questioning whether this author is just a rich wanker, then let me give you some insight into my wee life.

I was raised in Australia by immigrant Maltese parents who believed in dreams. My mother was a machinist and my father, a cleaner. In short: no money, no fancy clothes, living in housing commission homes and budgeting to go on once-a-year holidays in a seaside house (which I now own) on Manly beach just thirty kilometres from home. I was educated; however, that is irrelevant. What I had from my parents was to believe in dreams and, with the exception of my mother, the notion that to hell with what other people thought.

A good start, but I had to create my own reality. I had realised through playing sport in Australia, particularly rugby league, that the mind cannot decipher between the surreal and the real, the subconscious and conscious, the rehearsal or the real play. Ian Thorpe, world champion swimmer, was constantly in the zone of high vibration whilst remaining calm. He has done the work both physically and visually before competing in the race. He then detached from the outcome because in his mind he had already broken the world record and swum the race before he dived into

---

11 Csikszentmihalyi, M. (1990). Flow: The psychology of optimal experience. New York, USA: Harper & Row Publishers.

the pool. This is one of the main reasons Australia, with a relatively small population of 26 million, dominates many world sports today.

This creative visualisation also became a part of my life at an early age. I played rugby league in my youth where I was told by my coaches to visualise my plays before the match. I had taken this advice one step further by ensuring that before falling asleep prior to a game I would rehearse my moves repeatedly in my head. I would end up dreaming the game plan in my head the night before the match. It became habitual and not unexpected that the same moves were executed on game day in exactly same way as the dream had turned out. I did the same prior to entering in swimming races where I represented Malta at the FISEC International games and New South Wales, Australia, in freestyle and butterfly in the seventies. I also applied visualisation to my studies, and to exams for the completion of my Bachelor of Business and MBA.

Also, thanks to my father, I was brought up as a recalcitrant Catholic, which meant I tended to do things I wanted without seeking permission and if required could ask for forgiveness later (Dad always said I could always go to confession any time I transgressed). This, I believe, made me more focused and free to choose my desired goals without conforming to a set of doctrines interpreted by the clergy of the day.

So, whilst my concept of an unlimited and non-prohibitive life cycle plan will appear to some as being over-the-top or fanciful, it happens to be my third plan. My first two plans have already been realised and therefore finalised. The only regret I had with the first two was that I set my sights *too low* and didn't really have the utmost faith in the law of attraction and of the theory of 'let go, let God', which is the Buddhist version of detachment. I was trying to *do* more and *control* more instead of *being* more. It's amazing how the Australian Aborigines and Native Americans knew about these secrets thousands of years ago. The Aborigine concept of

Dreamtime, which is the Australian Aborigine people's spiritual beliefs of existence, shows that they understood. It is believed that the spirits gave them their hunting tools and each tribe its land, their totems and their Dreaming. The Aboriginals believed by tapping into their ancestors' spirits made all things possible.

Now when I am in a difficult situation with money, I focus my very nervous and excited energy towards the feelings of abundance and joy. My decisions must emanate from a feeling of high, not low, negative vibrations. These are vibrations that make you feel so high that all you are concerned about is that precious moment. Some may say that I am turning to God, and I am. The aim is to turn every emotion into a feel-good emotion, so that the problem metaphysically dissolves. Once again, if you have difficulty in transitioning to the feel-good emotions, try faking it until you make it.

I had realised at a young age that actions or decisions based on or around negative emotions *always* led to poor outcomes. This is why I will *never* respond when things get heated or when people start to get emotional. If I have to walk away from the situation to establish the right feeling, I do. I may go out for a run, switch my mind to loving thoughts of my wife, or think of a perfect ski holiday or the new BMW. The main aim is not to focus on the problem, particularly when it doesn't feel right or the situation is uncomfortable. Gradually, my mood changes to positive, happy feelings and I am on a high towards the things I desire, not wasting counter-productive energy on the problem of lack of money or the things I haven't got. Then I have faith that the universe will provide the necessary resources and people to my flow of energy (let go, let God!). It works *all* the time.

As mentioned earlier, most people think about the lack of money rather than the abundance of money, therefore attracting through negative thoughts the opposite of what they would like to have, which is, of course, more money. This is another reason why most lottery winners lose all their winnings in a very short period of time. Once again, the problem is on the focus on money or the concern of losing it rather than feeling the flow of money towards a passionate, real purpose or desire.

Successful day traders on the stock markets understand this concept well. It is not whether you win or lose that counts, but the ability to put forward your best and develop the desire to continue to feel what the outcome will mean when it eventually comes. The majority of day traders from the dot-com days are no longer with us. This was a period where a drover's dog would have made money, it was that easy. However, when times got tough, particularly after September 11, we all heard the usual doomsayers' catchcries that the stock market is too risky, or, 'I'm out of here'. The truth is that day traders with the attitude and belief in the law of attraction actually made more money during the declared recession than before.

At the time of writing this book, the Dow dropped 800 points in three consecutive days. OK, let's put all this so-called airy-fairy stuff to the test. I just lost $250,000 on the stock market, right there and right then. The old Camilleri would have (to put it mildly) gone into a mind-blowing depression (when other people are losing money, it is a recession, when I am losing money, it is a depression), which would have consumed 98% of my thinking, feelings and actions. I would have probably sold to minimise my losses or just plunged myself into self-defeating self-pity. This, in turn, would have made me an unbearable grouch in front of my family and work colleagues.

So, true to the laws of attraction, I decided not to focus on the problem; rather, I would concentrate my feelings on the outcome of my investments. I mean really concentrate. I had to fake it to make it because the impulse to fall back into a doom and gloom mood was incredibly strong. I kept reinforcing my inner self and self-belief with a huge wallop of faith. I knew I had selected sound companies with strong fundamentals. I also reflected on the fact that my record of understanding trends and company balance sheets was pretty good. Therefore, I 'let go, let God', so the universe could take care of the outcome.

I continued to put the effort into feeling what it would be like for a few of my stocks to announce big contracts and maybe one to become subject to a takeover bid. I felt and imagined the joys of the mums and dads whose retirement would be more comfortable because of the rise in these stocks. My only regret now is that I limited the feelings to a few companies only.

The stocks rebounded by 1,000 points in two days, three new contracts were awarded and one of my stocks was indeed subject to a takeover bid. I was now $425,000 in front. Feel good? You bet. Coincidence? Well, after six favourable outcomes on similar situations like the one just given you, I don't care what you call it. My portfolio 12 months after the 800-point drop was at an all-time high of $1.2m.

Just remember that all things related to this planet must flow. It must be kept constantly moving or atrophy will set in, slowly but surely. If you vibrate your energies towards the lack of money, the universe will deliver exactly what you ask for. Remember: like feelings attract like wants. The universe will always answer your call. Call it prayer, call it mediation, call it quiet time, call it whatever you want. Just remember that your present thought sets you up for your next outcome. It is simply cause and effect.

This is why it is folly to get passionate or excited about obtaining money per se or as a stand-alone transaction. Especially when your old beliefs will have you focused on the lack of money or the thinking that the abundance of money is 'evil'. Either way, both are negative feelings. The first step on how to change your money beliefs is to gradually develop a feeling of excitement towards the wants or outcome the money can achieve as a means to an end, not an end in itself. Finally, allow the universe, or God, to produce things for you. Allow yourself to feel abundant in whatever you desire.

Do not focus on money; if you do, money will always elude you. Instead, focus on the feeling of the object or situation you desire and prepare to receive it.

As a brief note, it is highly recommended that you read the excellent *Rich Dad, Poor Dad* series of books by Robert Kiyosaki[12] on how to gain financial independence in a relatively short period of time.

Eckhart Tolle, in his fantastic book (some say bible) *A New Earth*, describes the paradoxical nature of money in outstanding detail. Tolle states that one's ability to detach and display non-resistance to what *is* is key to attracting abundance.[13] This display of 'surrender' or 'detachment' seems completely at odds with today's politically correct business world; however, it makes sense. Tolle speaks of 'surrender' as the ability to remove oneself from the egotistical mind and move towards your spiritual being or your true self. This state of consciousness gives you the ability to make informed decisions and to manifest 'things' according to your real purpose in life, not just material 'stuff' that fills your garage and share portfolio with short-term fulfilment or 'happiness'. The ego is *never* satisfied.

And finally, to avoid wasting many years of your life struggling with finances, like I did, I highly recommend that you read the previous passage again in order to *prepare* yourself for the financial success you deserve.

---

12 Kiyosaki, R. (1998). *Rich Dad, Poor Dad: What the rich teach their kids about money — that the poor and middle class do not!* New York, USA: Warner Books, Inc.

13 Hemachandra, R. (25 Sept, 2010). *Eckhart Tolle on making money, alignment with life, and the present moment* [blog]. Retrieved from https://rayhemachandra. com/2010/09/25/eckhart-tolle-on-making-money/.

5

Law of Attraction

What I focus on in life is what I get. And if I concentrate on how bad I am or how wrong I am or how inadequate I am, if I concentrate on what I can't do and how there's not enough time in which to do it, isn't that what I get every time? And when I think about how powerful I am, and when I think about what I have left to contribute, and when I think about the difference I can make on this planet, then that's what I get.

You see, I recognise that it's not what happens to you; it's what you do about it. —*W. Mitchell*[14]

The law of attraction cannot be created nor destroyed; it just is. Ask yourself why it is that some people seem to have riches and/or good health, while others don't. Why is it that some people have no problems or have an incredible laidback style and achieve their goals without effort? Well, the law of attraction works on the principle that like vibrations will be in harmony with other like vibrations. That is why what you ask for is what you get. It is that simple. However, consistency is the key. In good times or bad, the thoughts must be present in order to set you up for the next outcome. Successful people know to have positive thoughts of love and feelings all the time no matter what the present circumstances,

14 Goodreads. (2018). *W. Mitchell quotes*. Retrieved from https://www.goodreads.com/author/quotes/384462.W_Mitchell

as they know the only outcome from this practice is a positive one.

There is no deviation from this law. It won't be taught at universities or colleges, but the rich have been practising this law (some subconsciously) for years. Napoleon Hill, who made a life-time study of the effective habits of the then richest men in the world, concluded that it is probably the single biggest secret of the rich that ordinary people don't get but have at their disposal for free. Not only do the rich, according to Hill, set their sights on success by visualising it, they place themselves in a state of readiness like it has already happened. It is all about placing oneself in a state of *being* rather than *doing*.[15]

I frequently ask my sales people what it is they would like to *be* rather than *do* before engaging in a meeting with a prospect or customer. I get my sales people to feel for the desired outcome of the meeting before the meeting has commenced; it might be the feeling of having the 'success' bell ring in the office that a new deal has been won, or the joy the customer will receive when a completion of a successful project ensures a rapid promotion for the key sponsor. Or simply to grant them access to power because they know they can make a difference for the well-being of the company.

I do a lot of public speaking. Most people are amazed that I appear calm, well rehearsed and attentive during presentations. Most audiences feel that I am speaking directly to them on an individual basis and feel that I must have known the subject matter for years (when sometimes I only have twenty-four hours to prepare). It wasn't always like this. When people ask me how I do it, I reply that I always put my reality into a state of high positive vibration by feeling (empathising) for the audience I am presenting to. I empathise with my audience to the point that I am the audience, not just a presenter up there separate from the audience. I also feel that the presentation will be a success before

---

15 Hill, N. (2015). *Think and grow rich.* New York, USA: Chartwell Books.

delivering the speech. I imagine thoughts that the audience will be enlightened, educated and entertained. If I don't feel those emotions before the presentation, then I know my inner being is telling me that I am lacking in preparation for success. I then go back to basics by doing role plays and rehearsing in front of a make-believe audience (namely my dog, Kori). I need to prepare for the vision and get my feeling of success with my 'audience' to such a high level of ecstasy, that the outcome has to be successful. In fact, I should be able to make a fortune on this self-induced euphoria. Who needs drugs? It always works; success is guaranteed and, boy, do you have fun going through the process.

A friend of mine was appearing in front of 200 people in Galway, Ireland, as a stand-up comedian for the very first time. Most people who say that they'd rather die than present in front of a large audience do not know what it takes to capture an audience and have them spellbound in rapturous laughter for forty minutes, particularly when newcomers get booed and heckled for poor performances. Fiona had enormous powers to visualise the outcome of the presentation she was about to give. She *anticipated* the audience being pleased and laughing at her one-liners and wanting more. A successful outcome was achieved. Furthermore, during the break, many of the audience asked her where and when she was performing next – they didn't want to miss it. They didn't realise it was her first time.

In her fabulous book *Do Less, Achieve More*, Chin-Ning Chu tells the story of an evening in the 1960s when Clint Eastwood and Burt Reynolds were having dinner together. At that time, while Clint had already played major roles in several successful films and was recognised as an international star, Burt was still a struggling actor. Burt asked Clint how he had gotten his big break, and Clint answered: 'I prepared myself for success.'[16]

---

16 Chu, C. (1998). *Do less, achieve more: Discover the hidden power of giving in.* New York, USA: Harper Collins.

And remember what Ralph Waldo Emerson once said: 'What lies before you and what lies behind you are tiny matters compared to what lies within you.'[17]

Emerson and Eastwood, in my opinion, have experienced and expressed the transformation from the unconscious to the conscious by deliberately manifesting thought processes through to the creation of a desired outcome.

Some time ago I purchased a house that had a double carport that I didn't immediately need at the time of signing the contract for sale. I only had one car; however, my desire was to obtain two luxury cars. I deliberately created space for my desire by getting a double carport for the two luxury cars I had *not yet* obtained. I didn't need a double carport, but I desired two luxury cars. I realised I needed to prepare and feel for the space I was providing, so my wants would flow freely. I did not work out how I was going to pay for the cars. This is another pearl of wisdom that took me forty-three years to understand: you can be the director, scriptwriter, and actor in your life, but *one role you do not have to perform is that of the producer.* I knew that I had to create a vision and feeling that was real to me and allowed my energy to flow into the space I had created. In other words, I was creating my own reality. Later, the means of finance presented themselves in the form of bonus fees and a generous payout from an existing contract I did not directly plan for.

I firmly believe that if I did not have a desire for my cars and prepare to receive them, then the universe would have sidestepped me for someone who was.

I have also realised over time that if I had not created and surrounded myself from the outset with good professional and

17 Chandra, P. (18 Dec, 2012). *What lies behind us, and what lies before us, are tiny matters compared to what lies within us.* — *Ralph Waldo Emerson* [blog]. Retrieved from https://alwyzbpositive.wordpress.com/2012/12/18/what-lies-behind-us-and-what-lies-before-us-are-tiny-matters-compared-to-what-lies-within-us-ralph-waldo-emerson/

personal mentors, I would not have allowed myself to have both financial and physical wellness flow to me. So, I researched and searched (I really mean searched – expect to go through several candidates) for the right accountants, lawyers, financial planners, Pilate's teachers, swim coaches and successful business mentors.

The ability to create your *own* reality is so vitally important.

To focus on present norms and conformity is to surrender your life to one of everlasting mediocrity and underachievement. This point was illustrated to me quite vividly and by accident when I quite keenly took up a position of sales in the United Kingdom. I didn't realise at the time (the reasoning so obvious to everyone except me) that holidays in the northern hemisphere were taken during the July–August period (in Australia it is December–January), and as a consequence, the general consensus was that business tended to slow down and contracts were hard to close. Well, nobody had told me. I was not informed about this 'holiday downturn' until after the end of August when it was announced that we had just closed a *record* month in the firm's seventeen-year history. My reality was that business continued as usual during this period. What is *your* reality telling you now?

Another example of the power of the law of attraction in the work place came in the shape of a long and protracted series of negotiations with a company in the Netherlands. We were hoping to do well with this company in terms of employment and profits for our shareholders and employees. We knew we could deliver a world-class customer facing solution to the Dutch company. However, the manager in control of the project was a bono fide problem generator. At the time, I was working as the lead team member, negotiating to deliver technology and services to the Dutch company. Before, during and after the process, the PG continued to negotiate with our company as if the contract did not exist, which made us feel that we were constantly in a win/lose situation with this person. He kept saying he was 'feeling disappointed' every time we tried to deal with him. There were no facts to support his disappointment. He basically wanted everything for free. Well, from our point of view, this approach was not sound grounds for commercial viability.

Over a period of five months, the PG continued to block, cajole, transfer guilt and play games; he didn't wish to compromise on anything, and at the extreme, put a halt to the project to make his point. We also played our role in the emotional negative payoff game by seeking revenge at every opportunity. We documented everything. We were in a good shape to win a legal battle if one eventuated. However, what I began to notice was that we were treating the PG in exactly the same 'parent–child' manner as he was treating us; we had created an impasse based on mutual distrust. This was obviously compounded by our manner of communication and our feelings of negativity towards the PG – we had nothing positive to say about our Dutch protagonist, even to the extent that on one of our single malt nights with our CEO, we were having 'fun' at the Dutchman's expense by attempting to teach a smart border collie how to do 'business' on the PG's leg when he was to arrive in our offices the following week. The collie was smarter than us – he refused to play.

The feeling of negativity towards this PG was so strong that we didn't realise that we were attracting exactly what we asking for. We were not progressing forward with any meaningful compromise or workable solutions. I then tried to deal with the PG by using the techniques I have explained in this book. However, I soon realised that even though I knew this would be effective with me and the PG on a one-on-one basis, I needed to establish a continued balance of harmony with my all my work colleagues (we needed all to be on the same page), otherwise, yes, you guessed it, another PG would simply take his place.

So, I gathered the team around and we started to look and feel for positives in the project and the rest of the people associated with the Dutch company. We made an impressive list: they were excellent programmers, good project managers, the work that they had performed to date was exemplary, and the Dutch CEO was very reasonable. We started to feel that we were all part of an exciting new project that would provide outstanding customer benefits. We were all feeling like co-creators instead of co-destroyers. We kept feeling that way no matter what the PG threw at us in terms of unreasonableness.

Well, as mentioned before, the law of attraction *never* fails. Within a week, the PG suddenly and miraculously went on five weeks annual leave. The timing was amazing, given the critical stage of the project and the seniority of the PG (most senior executives rationalise that if you can afford to take five weeks leave, then your position may be jeopardy). The PG was replaced by the most affable and reasonable project director you could hope to find in the information technology industry. The result was that the whole proof of concept, which until now had taken nine months under the PG, was delivered within nine days.

It is worth noting that not only were we paid for a successful proof of concept, we were also granted additional project work to the tune of €500,000, and the customer remained an exemplary reference for future prospects. Three months later, the project was generating €50,000 per month in consulting fees. The PG, whilst still having PG characteristics, was now in line with the energy of the rest of the team and posed no problem or threat to us.

Another story from recent events further highlights the concepts of PG issues and paradigm shifts. We decided to put our villa up for sale in Queenstown, New Zealand. From day one, my mistake was to place the listing with the established real estate agents and ignore my inner self telling me to place the sales engagement with the '1% real estate agents', a stereotype term used (sometimes in derogatory sense) to describe real estate agents that charge 1% (as opposed to the establishment charging 4% plus) commission on the sales price achieved for their clients. They are able to do this by using a different business model from the traditional, established, 'bricks and mortar' real estate companies. However, by initially signing with two established real estate agents, we had wasted four anxious months with zero results – not even an offer. Also, just about everyone around us – other villa owners, the property managers, neighbours and interestingly enough other 'traditional' real estate agents – all said that the price *we* had in mind of $1.2m was impossible to obtain. The figure *they* had in mind was no more than $1.1m, and most said $1m was the probable outcome. Well, be careful of your thoughts – we received and accepted an offer of $1,205,000. Also, we believe that what added to the result of achieving this record sales price for our villa was acting on the edict of 'selling when you don't have to sell'. Most people unfortunately sell assets when they are placed in an environment of desperation. Examples of reasons of 'need to sell' may be an increase in interest rates, bridging finance, excessive debt, loss of a job, inability to service the loan, divorce, and so on. This adds to their fear-based emotions and creates negative thoughts; the universe picks up this energy and you will know by now where this is leading: negative thoughts equal negative outcomes!

My wife and I continued to set goals. However, as in the example above, we have realised that through a combination of our own and other people's fears, we were, in effect, creating our own internal PG energy. This was limiting our potential to do bigger and brighter things. It is a struggle. We continue to move on to the next 'thing' when we start doubting ourselves or have negative people around us. We are tough on ourselves when we start judging others and their situations. We remind ourselves that every human thought and action is based on either fear or love. Nothing happens by accident in God's world. You and others around you will determine your circumstance.

So, we must choose to focus our energies on the love of what we want to desire, not the negative energy of fear.

Real-Life Case Study

I was at another crossroad in my life whilst writing this book. I had just been relieved of my duties at a high-paying job (i.e. terminated). The future was uncertain. We were, at the time, asset rich, but cash poor (all our money was locked in growth investments with no income). I had realised subconsciously that the job was about to end six months earlier – it just didn't feel right and my energies were down. So, the outcome of being asked to go, in all truthfulness (even though it hurt like hell at the time) did not come as a surprise. The major lesson of life for me was to try and bring the subconscious world to the surface; we had to begin to feel with our soul and use our brains to act as a performance tool of intelligence, not the other way around. So, right then I was more aware than ever on how 'things' work. I knew that if I planned for the future and acted on the plan in the present, then my theory would work. So, as a real-life exercise, I commenced to practice and journal what I preach. I hope this process will give you an example of the practical approach of asking for what we deserve to the universe.

Together with my wife we listed our goals as follows:

Goals

- Eliminate $810,000 NAB loans by 31/03/04

- Reach $1.2m in shares by 31/03/04

- Join CSI corporation to earn $1m per annum by 30/09/04

- Receive $340,000 in commissions from GT by 1/3/04

- Invest in two property trusts by 30/06/04

- Earn $320,000 income per year from investments

- Do a minimum of thirty minutes of exercise every day

- Pray, read spiritual books and pick a motivation card and follow its advice each day

- Be closer to Elliot, Bethany and Elisabeth (children)

We wrote these goals in the form of affirmations each day. I recorded each day's progress in my journal and continued to write the affirmations that gave me the biggest buzz.

My daily affirmations (handwritten twice a day) were:

- **Affirmation #1**: I am financially free to explore my true purpose. I am currently earning over $325,000 per year.

- **Affirmation #2**: There is no such thing as luck. Nothing ever happens by chance. Everything, good or bad, that comes into your life is there as the result of the unvarying, inescapable Law of Being. And the only operator of that law is none other than *yourself*.

- **Affirmation #3**: I am with the Divine Spirit. I am the child of life. In life I live, so I have no fear. I am surrounded by the peace of the universe and all is well. I am not afraid of people; I am not afraid of things; I am not afraid of circumstances; I am not afraid of myself, for my ancestors and spirit are with me. The peace of life fills my soul, and I have no fear. In the presence of life, no fear can touch me.

- **Affirmation #4**: I am not afraid of the past; I am not afraid of the present. I am not afraid for the future, for the Spirit is with me.

Journal

This is daily journal tracked and recorded all events that impacted me both quantitatively and qualitatively. I also look back on the journal to acknowledge and feel gratitude for what has occurred.

Day 1:

Received £400 for insurance refund.

Received $340,000 in commissions from GT.

Received a lovely email from customers and partners regarding departure.

Due to advance payments, the bank reduces monthly repayment by $400 per month.

Day 2:

Vicki sells goods for £110.

Shares rise by 10%.

Changed removalist – save $200.

Head-hunter calls for a meeting.

Day 3:

Offshore bank offers new competitive tax saving product.

Sold water system for £80.

Day 4:

Shares flat.

Move is flowing freely.

Refund of £200 from electricity utility.

Vicki sells more stuff for £35.

Day 25:

> Completely debt free.
>
> Income is now $125,000 per annum from investments.
>
> Consultancy contracts signed for $50,000 for two days per month.

Day 40:

> Property trusts have appreciated by 100%.
>
> Purchased another property trust for $300,000 with 8.1% yield.
>
> Good month from passive income – approaching $6,000 per month.
>
> Purchased fine wines for $10 per bottle – retail $18.

Day 42:

> Refund cheque from UK Inland Revenue of £621.76.

Further affirmations based on the journal:

- Affirmation #5: I am financially free. I am so grateful. Abundance is flowing freely every day. I am earning over $325,000 per year in passive income.

- Affirmation #6: I am on purpose, therefore I am financially free earning $325,000 per year being who I want to be.

The task of manifestation is new to most people. Most just give up and place their hands in fate. Maybe it takes a trip back to nature and to just simply *be* to get back to who you really are. My advice is to persevere.

The difficult task on the journey to achieve your goals is to say no to things and people around you. Especially when you don't know what is best for you. However, experience and gut feeling is what you must rely on here. If the universe keeps giving you abusive boyfriends or rotten bosses who just want to do you out of commissions, then say no. Watch out for early warning signs such as those from the list detailed under problem generators. Once you have cleared your nasty environment, then create a new one free of problems and issues. Fantasy? Well, it all depends whether you see life as having problems or simply one of challenges and/ or opportunities. Once again, it is your choice, your reality, your script and your life. Which movie do you want?

The next chapter will explain how.

6

Passion and Persistence

To have a negative and emotional focus on problems is wasted energy, which, if continued, will attract negative outcomes all the time. So why do it?

It is as simple as that. Try practising not being negative for five days straight and see if you can do it. If you stumble, go back to day zero and start again. This exercise will put you in the right frame of mind and energy to create what you want. This is why the rich are often heard saying, 'I don't see any problems, just opportunities.' And why they respond firmly to negative discussions by stating, 'Please don't bring me problems, just solutions.'

However, let me again make it clear that this is more than just positive thinking or supreme optimism. It is the gut-wrenching vibration, passion and feeling that gives you a constant focus without effort because you are in a continuous high-energy flow towards your wants. It is the ability to do less but to achieve more within your own reality or script that you alone are responsible for. It is this mindset that differentiates you from mediocrity. You and you alone will create your reality. This ability will give you the utmost control and freedom in your life.

As stated earlier, the process must be adhered to in order to achieve success. Though, as you know, it is hard to be in a constant feel-good frame of emotional bliss, particularly when the proverbial is about to hit the fan. Let me share with you a real-life example of when I faced a huge crisis that tested this faith.

I was a director of one of the best and most respected Scottish firms in the IT industry and it was facing the ultimate challenge by being squeezed into extreme financial difficulties. The pressure was on, big time. The bank was being utterly draconian by insisting on daily audits, high fees and management time, and insisting on weekly layoffs, causing staff fear. I have never in my career witnessed such unreasonableness or such a ruthless display of capitalism at its worst than by this particular bank. We were so focused on what the bank wanted, we were restricted in our selling efforts. Therefore, the root cause of the problem, the lack of sales, was being exacerbated by the actions of the moneylender. What made this action all the more incredulous and asinine was that the total net realisable fixed assets of the company, being bricks and mortar, totalled more than £5m. The overdraft we were seeking to operate effectively and pay wages was only £250,000. It didn't make any sense, but we were at the mercy of a bank, which had been burnt in the dot-com era and wanted out of the information technology industry all together. If we didn't bring in this £1.2m deal, the company would fold.

The old me would silently panic and think of the worst-case scenario, while at the same time wishing the deal would come in. But, with strong will and discipline (which I found was easier said than done), I went headlong into writing a new script with all the positive feel-good emotions I could muster.

I continued daily to repeat the following;

- This company will not only be a viable organisation, it will prosper to become one of the great companies in the world.

- The firm deserves worldwide recognition for its excellence in engineering and customer satisfaction.

- The employees will be ecstatic and in admiration of a great company.

- The Scottish press will write about the growth and meteoric rise of one of their own firms on the world scene.

- The locals will be proud to call this firm 'Scottish Excellence'.

- Many deals will materialise in the months of October, November and December 2002.

- It will be 'natural' for the firm to close £2m deals every month.

- The deals will enable the firm to grow in Holland, Germany, France and USA.

- Banks will clamour to be involved with the firm.

- The owners will deserve all the rewards and accolades bestowed upon them.

- We are moving towards the personal goal of financial independence.

When I repeated the above script, my energy and emotions would just feel so good. I could taste it, smell it and, more importantly, see it become a reality. I didn't know what the process would be, but I would focus on the above script and 'let go, let God'. It was just amazing how my mood would change when the mantra was repeated. I thoroughly believed it would all be fine. I was on a high.

I will tell you what happened over the next four weeks.

Those four weeks were both frustrating and euphoric. It was an incredible journey. A Buddhist believes that one must enjoy the journey in order for one to appreciate the outcome. Well, at that time, I definitely needed more practice to be convinced.

Initially, as expected, the proverbial had hit the fan. It did not go as smoothly as anticipated or desired. I had incredible down days when things were not going well at all. Negatives were flowing in at a million miles an hour and from all directions – delays in contracts, difficult negotiations, stock market falls, staff and family issues, bank pressures, personal debt and more. I was continually changing my focus off these negative issues onto the feel-good vibes, concentrating on the script above. Boy, this was hard.

A deal was taken away from us at least three times before an agreement in principle had been reached. However, it was not an unconditional contract. The bank would not accept it as a solid invoice for payment. More work (or positive vibrating) had to be done. The 'faith meter' had to be primed and fed. All the other opportunities that had been earmarked to close, didn't. We would go two steps forward, then three steps back. We had to continue to focus on what it would feel like to close these deals. It was very difficult not to go into panic mode and force the outcome. This was definitely the hardest thing for me to do – let go, let God. I had been so used to expecting and controlling outcomes, and when they didn't materialise, I would go into fear and sometimes depression. I kept on reading the script and learnt for the first time in my life what faith was all about. It was tough, especially when I had others around me crying doom and gloom. The CEO and CFO were focusing on and trying to deal with neolithic banks and socialistic councils. Every deal in the pipeline was slipping. Furthermore, at the same time, a huge deal in Holland had to be pushed back from a silly price list that had been presented to the company on our behalf two years before. This pricelist was fifty percent lower than the proposal we tabled. We had a builder with a court order to seize assets if payment was not made by December 2002. We could not re-bank until the council would allow us to lease the building we had owned, and we could not re-bank unless sales were deemed bona fide for invoicing. However, we refused to give these areas of concern any attention. I also learnt that any display or partaking of any negative emotions from anywhere or anyone during this period would continue to feed fear, uncertainty or doubt. It is so important that you keep positive and motivated people around you during stressful times. I remember reading this apt quote at the time:

> Anxiety and fear produce energy. Where we focus that energy noticeably affects the quality of our lives. Focus on the solution, not the problem. —*Walter Anderson*[18]

Well, not only did we secure the huge £1.2m deal from the huge Dutch telecommunications company (remember earlier how we had changed our whole attitude towards the Dutch market), we also secured revenues from audit procedures, council grants and other minor but important sales orders. The big surprise was an approach by a venture capitalist firm to invest in our growth to the tune of £4m. Even little opportunities that were adding up to hundreds of thousands of dollars came in for the month of November. Bloody fantastic! However, let me remind you once again that this process was difficult and uncomfortable. The temptation to panic and take control and force an outcome is extremely high, but it is necessary for you to persevere so that you may obtain confidence and faith in the laws of creation, which you should realise by now, *are solely within you.*

It also pays to commit to write down specific goals on paper every day until the goal is reached. As Brian Tracy once remarked, 'An average person with average talent, ambition and education can outstrip the most brilliant genius in our society, if that person has clear, focused goals.'[19]

18 Quotefancy. (n.d.). *Anxiety and fear produce energy. Where we focus that energy noticeably affects the quality of our lives: focus on the solution, not the problem.— Walter Anderson*. Retrieved from https://quotefancy.com/quote/1578590/ Walter-Anderson-Anxiety-and-fear-produce-energy-Where-we-focus-that-energy-noticeably

19 Goodreads. (2018). *Brian Tracy*. Retrieved from https://www.goodreads. com/quotes/629391-an-average-person-with-average-talent-ambition-and-education-can

The method to ensure you have a single focus is called **BUMS**.

Be specific of the definition of the goal you wish to set. As an example: I wish to finalise a sales contract with XYZ by November 2003.

Underline the fact that you must commit yourself to writing this goal daily until it is achieved.

Make yourself feel the image of attaining your goal. Believe you already have it in your possession. Use meditation or imagery methods to visualise the feeling of the item or spiritual thing you want. Do it daily or whenever you feel negative. Remember: fake it until you make it. Get an old deposit book and write in the amounts of your daily deposit until the amount is achieved and then write a cheque to pay off the mortgage or obtain the item.

Set achievement rewards when the item manifests. For example, after endless hours of practice, tennis players make a fist when they have made a good passing shot in a real match. If you pay off your mortgage early, then go out to dinner and have a huge feast. Celebrate your wins and acknowledge that you have created the outcome and circumstance, and luck had nothing to do with it.

During any period of despair or turmoil, it is essential to focus on what makes you feel good. Crabhorn refers to the practice of flip switching to a level of high-energy state of emotion in order to remain on track.[20] Be patient and enjoy the journey. Do not continually keep score. Remember, goals should keep you

20 Grabhorn, *Excuse me, your life is waiting.*

motivated. Don't focus on goals set by someone else for you. Have the faith and knowledge that you control your life. As philosopher Chuang Tzu explains in his poem *The Need to Win*:

When an archer is shooting for fun

He has all his skill.

If he shoots for a brass buckle

He is already nervous.

If he shoots for a prize of gold

He goes blind

Or sees two targets –

He is out of his mind.

His skill has not changed,

but the prize divides him.

He cares.

He thinks more of winning

Than of shooting –

and the need to win

Drains him of power.'[21]

Furthermore, have faith that a positive outcome will arrive; otherwise you will have a tendency to quit too soon. Remember the importance of passion and desire towards your goals. Motivation is the buzz of excitement you get when the passion and desire stirs within you to achieve *your* worthy goal.

---

21 Archon, S. (n.d.). *Inspirational Taoist Quotes and Stories by Chuang Tzu*. Retrieved from https://theunboundedspirit.com/inspirational-taoist-quotes-and-stories-by-chuang-tzu/

What did I learn? Besides a rapid understanding (for the first time) on the meaning of faith and the focus on a worthy goal, I learned *perseverance.* I had been taught to take the good with the bad, the ups with the down, and I was educated to take the economic busts with the booms. Previously, if I had concluded a good sale or made a huge profit on a share market trade, I would tend to rest on my laurels but feel helpless when the inevitable 'low' would come. Successful people don't view life that way. They see every circumstance as an opportunity to have abundance and happiness, be that spiritual and/or material. They chip away until the desired outcome is reached. They don't panic because they know if they put effort into the right actions and feelings, no matter what the circumstance, their dreams will manifest.

If you wish to know your past life, look to your present circumstances. If you want to know your future life look to your present actions! —*Buddha*

As mentioned, perseverance is key. 'You cannot improve one thing by 1000% but you can improve 1000 little things by 1%.' Jan Carlzon was the CEO of the SAS Group (Scandinavian Airlines) in 1981–1994 and turned the airline around from one of the industry's worst performers to one of its best. In doing so he revolutionized the airline industry through an unrelenting focus on customer service quality.[22]

I had also learnt during this period that it is important to keep changing your thoughts, vocabulary and behaviour towards appreciation and *joy* of your worthy goal.

How does this work on the metaphysical level? Well, remember that energy can never be created nor destroyed, and therefore

---

22 Keating, S. (26 May, 2016). *Small changes, big differences* [blog]. Retrieved from https://stevekeating.me/tag/success-in-little-things/

it must be allowed to flow into a particular state of readiness to determine its resting place. For example, the only difference between water (H_2O), ice (H_2O) and steam (H_2O) is the amount of heat energy (vibration) one applies to H_2O. Thus, the level of vibration determines the physical form of water, ice and steam much in the same way as your feelings are processed through your highly developed brain and nervous system to determine the manifested form that you have projected and felt for in your being.

This is why the single most important change of conditional thinking you must try to overcome is that you are not a victim of circumstance, but the human creation of energy from within that affects and attracts other forms of energy recipients from outside the body. You must come to grips with the fact that you are energy with the universe, not separate from it, it's people, God or any other form. It is all of you and at the same time none of you.

This is such a hard concept for most people to fathom because through time we have eliminated dreams and are told to suppress our true feelings. We have been made to feel guilty by others, particularly by their interpretation of laws, both spiritual through scriptures and legislatively through parliaments. We have lost the desire to feel for our dreams, and we have often had them replaced with a thinking process and procedures that have generally been created by others for their *own* purposes. We can often see this marvel in the faces of children before they enter preschool (preconditioning). The joy and happiness of exploring the outer boundaries of their comfort zone and discovering new ways to amuse themselves is a delight to be seen. In the same way, have you ever noticed that the older people get, the more child-like they become in their nature and character? The bottom line is that these two groups of people (those aged five and under and those over sixty-five years old) are generally more content and happier than the massive group of ages that lie in between.

Therefore, be like a kid, or kid-like. Get out of worrying by remembering that to focus on negative emotions only leads to negative outcomes. One of my favourite quotes of all time summarises this sentiment exactly:

I've suffered a great many catastrophes in my life. Most of them never happened. —*Will Rogers*[23]

A technique to help you here is to always remain in a state of gratitude. As the quote above highlights, 'catastrophes' rarely happen, so be grateful for what you have. The paradox here is that you will receive more of what you are grateful for rather than cursing what you haven't got. Make a daily note of the big and small things that have come your way, and rejoice that you and the universe made it happen.

Gratitude is paramount in making sure you place yourself in the right frame of reference. This is especially important as you collect and horde 'toys and stuff' such as nice furniture, cars, clothes, books, TVs, etc. You tend to take all this for granted. However, look around at your 'stuff' and try to remember the feeling you had when you bought it. Be grateful that you have it now.

---

23 Rogers, W. (n.d.). *Will Rogers quotations*. Retrieved from http://ciscohouston. com/docs/docs/quotes/rogers.html

7.
Establishing the Emotional Umbilical Cord

I have made it a business practice and a family motto to always treat people and deal with them with respect. This respect must be mutual. No matter how good the deal may appear, if the human element of life and passion is missing from both sides, simply don't get involved or do business with that person or company. Believe me, you will be rewarded a hundred-fold in money and joy. Even now in 'retirement', I preface all my commercial dealings with trade and professional folk, including car dealers, real estate agents, bankers, plumbers and electricians with the statement that I am not after a *transaction* but a *business relationship*. I expect the business relationship to be for the long term with repeat business if required.

During a business relationship, I endeavour to find out a lot about the person: their interests, family, hobbies, sport, etc. I don't do this to manipulate or persuade people to my way of thinking. It's about genuinely understanding what the other side truly wants and what drives them in life. I can then concentrate on what's important to them and not waste their (or my) time. I am looking for a win/win engagement that benefits both parties. It also adds value to people's lives and your own if you truly listen intently and offer a benefit that serves their life's purpose. I call this developing the emotional umbilical cord.

I remember being told the story of a man sitting peacefully reading his daily newspaper in a train somewhere in New York city when quite suddenly and abruptly he was rudely disturbed by young group of kids making a loud racket and jumping all over the train. Now, this may seem like a form of behaviour that is not out of place in a city like New York. However, what made this situation so disturbing was that the children's father was present and totally oblivious to the behaviour of his kids. One of the passengers was furious and said out loud in front of the packed train that the man's children were a disgrace and should be kept under lock and key. The father then turned to the angry man with what could be described as a serene and saucer-eyed look, and said, 'Oh, I am terribly, terribly sorry. I didn't realise what they were doing. You are absolutely right. I will put a stop to it immediately.' A sigh came from the father, and then he continued. 'You see, they just went to see their mother in the hospital an hour ago, and complications set in and my wife, their mother, suddenly passed away. I suppose this is their way of reacting to the situation. I am deeply sorry that they have disturbed you.'

To assume to know how to judge behaviour will consistently make an ass out of you and me (ass–u–me). To be judgemental is a waste of time and energy. It places your focus on poor assumptions being made about individuals. This will eventually lead to poor outcomes in your own life. So why do it in the first place? Do not prevent the universe from providing people in your life that are there to help you achieve your dreams. To discount your fellow human being before really getting to know him or her could be the singularly most stupid thing you could do in your life. To learn not to judge could be the most important lesson you may receive out of this book.

8.

The Unnatural Organism

The unnatural organism is defined as an organisation that has, through its incorporation, developed and based its cultural and behavioural DNA on the motives of fear and greed rather than on improving society through ethical practices and reasonable profits. By making you consciously aware of what the real agenda is behind corporate strategy and tactics, this book will hopefully prepare you for the emotional highs and lows you are likely to encounter during your career.

Though I have retired from corporate life, I am not retiring from a life of making money or venturing into other business or life endeavours. My corporate experience and understanding of human behaviour in the unnatural organism has placed me in a good position to share from my perspective all those experiences with others, so new recruits may be consciously aware of what the corporate world is really all about.

It took two decades of saving and investing to enable my family to obtain financial freedom. We are currently drawing over $325,000 of passive income per annum. I am living with my wonderful, healthy family in picturesque Lake Hayes near Queenstown, New Zealand. Not bad for a former Toongabbie boy from the western suburbs of Sydney, Australia, where English textbooks like *Use Your Imagination* were used to carry our dope in.

The next part of the book is a guideline and / or an encyclopedia of the mistakes in dealing with corporate people from a humanistic point of view. As stated above, it is intended to prepare the young sales manager, business unit manager or managing director-in-waiting of the mythical benefits and irrational behaviours of working within a corporate structure.

The Corporate 'Kool Aid'

First of all, don't be fooled into believing all the corporate hoopla and cultural emphasis on objectives and mission statements – the corporate 'kool aid'. *You are a number,* and unless you believe in the tooth fairy or you are mediocre in the way you approach your job (more about that later), you will be retrenched and terminated many times during your corporate career. Don't get me wrong, many people have made good careers by being mediocre and learning how to survive the unnatural organism. This statement is not meant to be disparaging to those who have mastered the 'organism'. In fact, I have come to respect and admire those people who have survived and thrived in corporate structures. The intention here is to make you aware of what, in my experience, is reality in the way the corporate world behaves and acts towards its employees.

Therein lies the first observation: the employee. You are, whether you like it or not, just an 'employee', so unless you own a good block of corporate shares or are in the inner circle of management, you will be treated as an employee – you will be strictly measured on KPIs – and the notion of what you think a good and loyal employee is should therefore be negated and buried as just that: a noble thought. You are simply viewed as a number in the corporate world – you either make your quota or KPIs, or you are out.

This is a very important first lesson to learn. If you don't realise that corporations fundamentally strategise and behave for greed (profit) and fear (loss), you will be suckered into thinking that you are important. The corporation is a ruthless and unemotional beast that will reward the individual that meets – not exceeds – targets (more on this later). The corporation will make life hell for those that don't meet targets with inevitable termination of employment.

Therefore, please recognise that the corporation should be treated as a *vehicle* to get you where you wish to be: making money or developing skill sets. Unless you own the majority of shares, the corporation is not to be treated as a passionate, sincere, forgiving and reasonable organism.

Most IT corporations I have worked for (particularly those listed on NASDAQ) are dominated by one overriding objective, and that objective is *money*. In some people's eyes there may be nothing wrong with that; however, firms will go into the psychology (brainwashing) of what it wants by using 'motivating' techniques with its employees in order to achieve its goals. This chapter will reveal what these techniques are so that you may be consciously aware and know what they do and how to deal with them.

The Work Christmas Party

Oh boy, this is one day of the year you should avoid or at least be on your best behaviour – and definitely watch the alcohol consumption. Having been a manager and sat on various remuneration boards, I can tell you that I have seen more people suffer the consequences of bad/stupid behaviour at the work Christmas party than from any other day of the year.

I have seen hard-working individuals (for 364 days of the year) miss out on promotions, pay rises, and end-of-year awards and trips simply by not understanding the impact of their actions on this one festive day.

Things to remember and watch out for:

- Don't kid yourself: this festive day will always be a work event, *not* a social event.

- Avoid flirting (especially with the boss's partner – sounds obvious but alcohol does deaden the brain cells and makes people do stupid things).

- Don't forget that senior management will have an eye on you not matter how many jokes are shared around.

- Your first (maybe your last) bad social impression with your colleagues and management will stick with you throughout your career.

- Leave early and don't do 'after parties'. Especially for 'risqué' events. An example I remember all too well is when a managing director (and close friend) of a firm I was working for invited a select few attendees at an events party to go to a strip club (it was his birthday after all) after the event had officially closed. Word got around of the 'after party' and the select few became many. The very next day the same managing director had a call from an irate CEO of a company whose staff had been participating at the event to complain voraciously that such an invitation (even though they were not officially invited) created a human resources nightmare for him, as many of his staff were offended and complained. *Don't* do 'after parties'!

- Do not hang around with one particular group – socialise with everyone. You may not know or be aware of who is in the inner circle of power or influence. It's best to cover all bases by socialising with different groups.

Regular Social Gatherings

Simply put and very similar to the Christmas party: *avoid them!*

For the last fifteen years I have politely declined to go for 'drinkies' in a social workplace setting.

Once again, there is no such thing as 'social' in the workplace environment. The games people play are too vast and comprehensive for you to take on the risk. Generally, these gatherings tend to be 'bitch' sessions. Don't be fooled into thinking that what you may or may not say won't get back to a particular source or influence of power who will blame you as the instigator or think you are in some way associated with any rumour that may be circulating. The perception that may form (which becomes reality in senior managements' eyes) can be detrimental to your career. You will do well to avoid.

An item of discussion that should be avoided at social gatherings besides politics, religion and sex are share tips. Learning the hard way that share tips should be avoided puts you in a 'no-win' situation even when your 'tip' goes up in price. Share tips can create a long-term PG scenario for you. For example, you may give a passionate buy signal on your favourite stock to a colleague, or worse, to a customer, and the next day or week the price goes into free fall rather than increasing ten-fold in price like you said it would. You will be hounded regularly to explain the drop in price, or worse, you will be asked the question whether they should 'average down' by buying more at these 'low' prices before your predicted ten-fold hike happens. If this is a customer, good luck trying to sell to him or her in the future, as all they are seeing when a meeting is called (if you manage to get one) is: this is the person who has lost me a lot of money. And, as stated earlier, the PG situation is still there even if you happen to be correct and the price does go up ten-fold. Why? Because the next question they will ask you is, 'At what price should I sell?' Now you are getting to see the 'no-win' scenario. If you tell them to sell at say 100% increase and it goes up 300%, you will still be tagged with the image of selling too early and not making an extra 200% profit for them, or if you do tell them to sell at a 100% increase but the share does not hit the target price and goes down to where they are 'only' making a 50% increase, you will still be tagged in their minds as someone who lost them money when they should have made more.

As I said above, share tips are best avoided.

The Sales 'Kick-off' Conference

Commonly referred to as the 'kool aid' or 'ra ra' sessions, the annual sales conference is where corporate executives attempt to 'brainwash' you into thinking that their company, culture and objectives are the best thing that has ever happened to your life. Just as at the Christmas party, you must be on high alert and on your best behaviour. Do not treat this as a 'jolly' to have fun and get plastered.

In short, this is where corporate executives attempt to play 'God' with your life. They seek your unconditional commitment and motivation to the goal of profit targets and market share. Whilst this behaviour is common among most companies, what you need to be aware of is the unbridled hype and hubris that underlines the company's agenda. As before, you are basically a number, an asset to deliver outputs that the company wants, even though the company vehicle may not be set up in terms of infrastructure or product development to support your sales effort. The company may be missing a wheel or two or even a motor to help you to achieve their objectives, but if you dare raise this as an issue, you will be viewed as negative at best or as a problem at worst. Remember, the unnatural organism will never ever face up to reality (until management changes or it goes bankrupt). I have been in situations where after six years in business our company achieved one hundred percent market share in our territory (i.e. we had sold to every identified customer in our area). There were simply no further customers available to sell to (even for cross- or upselling). Even so, the unnatural organism wanted their ubiquitous fifteen percent growth. Go figure!

There was another time when we were establishing a new market in Japan. Unfortunately, in the first year of our sales penetration, Japan was struck by its worst tsunami in the country's history. However, the very next day and true to form, the unnatural organism, after giving politically correct and insincere platitudes to all that would listen, wanted to know and demanded how we were going to make our targets for the coming year!

The Budget Process

I must say, having participated in this corporate function for the last thirty-five years, I have come to the conclusion that the budget process is a complete *waste of time.*

Why? Because senior management have already, from the beginning of the process, decided or at least formed a firm idea of the figure in their head of what the targets are to be. However, Harvard or Stanford tells them that senior management should have everyone participating in the process so the lowest to the highest ranked individual has ownership and accountability for 'their' budget.

How to 'play your role' in the budget process:

- Appear enthusiastic and willing to participate (which is what management expects you to do).
  - Find out what management has in mind from the get-go and work towards this figure.

  - Do not take a contrarian or realistic view of the budget – you will be deemed to be negative and viewed as a non-team player. For example, I recall the time when my dear friend Ross had put in a copious amount of time and effort into a fantastic PowerPoint presentation highlighting the challenges and solutions together with the resultant budget required to execute *his* plan. It was a brilliant piece of strategic and tactical planning; however, because the plan was *his* not management's it was ignored and Ross was told to focus on the current corporate objectives and plans. Even though he was asked to participate in the process, he was ostracised for being a 'show pony' and a contrarian. Ironically, over the following years we noticed many parts of Ross's original presentation filter down in the planning process. The difference being it was now deemed to be management's idea not *his*.

- Don't waste time on this process (life is too short). I have wasted twelve months of my life over a thirty-year period that I will never get back 'doing' budgets. Management will always get you to accept their figures.

- Never be a superstar and say you can achieve more or that the budget is too low – remember, mediocrity, not superstars, survive long-term in the corporation.

- Also remember that in business (and in life) you don't get what you deserve but what you negotiate. Don't sweat the small stuff when negotiating anything. Remember that 'to win the war you may need to lose some battles'. Therefore, try to focus on the big, long-term objective. What will help you is to swallow and keep in check 'the ego' and the emotive outburst associated with thinking you are the centre of the universe.

- Furthermore, when dealing with people, 'play the ball not the man'. If you get into any emotional stoush with people, it is better to walk away than to win the 'battle' that the ego loves to win. These wins are only temporary. I repeat: remember and focus on the long-term objective.

Conference Calls

I have wasted five years of my life over my entire career on the ubiquitous conference call. When you are over fifty, you realise this wasted time just makes you so angry, as you can never get it back.

It is amazing how many employees justify their working (existence) day by saying how many conference calls they have been on. I have generally witnessed very little action or output derived from the activity, other than the setting up of another conference call. In my experience, most conference calls are just there to air grievances or discuss problems. Very few produce a solution.

The seasoned conference call attendee(s) who knows how to play the unnatural organism will tend to just listen and add very little to the discussion. Over time, I have recognised that this is a smart tactic.

The key observations from these seasoned colleagues on conference calls are as follows:

- Insist that an agreed agenda is issued prior to the meeting and that minutes are taken immediately after the meeting. (Refuse to attend if an agenda is not issued.)

- Never volunteer for action items – unless they are directly related to you earning money or career advancement. Beware of requests that are outside your terms of employment and bonus structure; you generally become 'cheap labour' for other people's agenda items that are not important for your career or your hip pocket.
  — Volunteering will consume a lot of your time and energy away from what you are measured on and paid to do.

  — Volunteering will tend to have you owning the problem, whilst others (if the outcome is successful) take the glory. If you fail, you will fail alone. Remember: Success has many fathers and mothers; failure has just one orphan!

- At the appropriate time and sprinkled with a good sense of humour, nominate someone else who is on the call to own the action item. If they are successful, you can claim part ownership and merit for the 'joint' outcome.

- Use the 'mute' button during the conference call. This prevents you from inadvertently saying something inappropriate or making comments that are irrelevant.

- Never be late for conference calls. Be respectful; show up on time.

Email Responses

In general, *do not respond to emails immediately*. At best, you can become a slave to the electronic forms of correspondence that will eventually distract you from your objectives or, at worst, you write something that you may regret later on. So, in general, *don't* respond to emails, especially immediately, and especially if the content within the email makes you emotional. A colleague I knew used to set up the 'delay send' function in Microsoft Outlook for at least twelve hours. He told me that he either amended or deleted over half of the pending emails before they were sent.

Also, I have often found that if something is so important, a person will pick up the phone and call you. In regard to emails, the delete button has become my favourite key on the keyboard. Up to ninety percent of my emails get the delete treatment. My basic rule is that unless it is related to customers, sales or reducing costs, the email is not important to me. I have never known anyone to be fired for not answering any other type of email. If it is *not* going to have an impact on your hard targets, then why do it?

Only under corporate necessity (e.g. budgets, etc.) and then only when requested three times will I respond to emails outside the basic rule.

Basic rules relating to email responses:

- Practice hitting the delete key to rid yourself of emails that don't deserve your attention or serve *your* objectives.

- Practice responding to critical emails by picking up the phone.

- Do not respond to emails that are emotionally charged. Wait at least twelve hours.

- Do not write anything that is disparaging or scathing of another employee or your management. Your work email is *not* secure; the company has a right to search its own database.

Also (and this has happened to me on two occasions), you may inadvertently send the disparaging email response to the person you criticised – extremely embarrassing and career-limiting.

- Do not write down your opinion or views on anything negative or condescending of a given process or system within your own organisation, even if it is justified. The paradox is that these types of emails are read by management as being negative, and if you are the author, you will be seen as becoming part of the problem even though you are with all good intent striving for a solution.

- Finally, if you are managing a team, please also insist that your staff refrain from writing negative or condescending emails. During one of my management roles I remember being accused by senior management of distributing an email criticising a member of staff based in the USA. The problem was, I didn't write it. Despite denials, I was tarred with the brush of descent and negativism. Unfortunately, mud sticks and perceptions remain. I was sacked two months later.

Presentation Skills

To play the game in the unnatural organism, a good presentation style and delivery is a must-have. I have seen average sales performers and other aspiring corporate executives be elevated above others in rank and remuneration simply because they had an above-average presentation style and delivery. It is essential that you learn the 'three Es': to Excite, Educate and Entertain an audience, both external and internal to your organisation. This will allow you to promote yourself in a highly effective manner. Learn from the best, take courses (e.g. through Toastmasters), plagiarise jokes (I used a lot from the great, late John Imlay), use statistics and, above all, put yourself out to be an expert. It is amazing how quickly you can elevate yourself to guru status in people's eyes by going around the public speaking circuit.

Good public presentation skills are also required for you to be recognised by head-hunters and senior executives of your competitors. During my career, I have been offered at least ten professional opportunities straight after my presentations. Obviously, when this happens you are in the 'box seat', as they are seeking you out.

I was fortunate to be employed by a good company that hired external consultants to help me sharpen up my presentations skills. These reputable professionals will analyse your style, pronunciation, mannerisms, facial expressions, hand movements, content, format and execution. I thought I was a pretty good speaker until these guys ripped me apart (leave your ego at home) and turned me into a reasonably good communicator. I will be forever grateful they did so.

Developing a Sense of Humour

The older and uglier I became as I moved through my senior years and towards the end of my career, the more I started to deliberately and methodically learn to develop a keen sense of humour. The main reason for this development was to help me deal predominantly with the stresses of corporate life. A good, healthy sense of humour helped me detach from the compounding and insistent irrational requests and nonsensical demands from management who essentially ran these unnatural organisms. Ironically, developing and consistently delivering a sense of humour around colleagues also had an interesting effect on management. I became the 'cool' or 'level-headed' member of staff and the one person that management came to in order to resolve issues they had with my peers or customers. I believe that by developing a sense of humour, I was viewed as irreverent but not irrelevant. They fathomed that if I could joke with fellow colleagues and peers in ugly situations that also relieved the tension in the room (particularly on conference calls) and generated laughter rather than angst, then I was seen as the person under control and in charge of the situation. As I said previously, my favourite word in the English language is 'paradox'.

A few common phrases I used continuously (which obviously need to be used in the right context) were as follows:

- It's like herding cats – used when simple matters are made complex.

- Now tell me how you really feel – used when someone goes into an over-the-top emotional rant.

- Do you have a shirt that goes with that tie? – used to break the ice when going into a known confrontational meeting.

- I really do love Americans, but I really can't eat a whole one! – used when American colleagues displayed too much hubris or arrogance.

The points above are just a few examples. The objective is to try and make fun of tense situations. There is also art in being a 'clown' that everyone loves rather than just appearing plain rude or cringeworthy. The main rule to follow is to never be vulgar or disparaging towards people.

Conclusion

To be frank, I didn't know how to start or finish this book. It all started out many decades ago as a diary of sorts. Notes to jolt down to keep me from going bonkers in the 'unnatural organism' world, or at best to help me to achieve clarity in dealing with problem generators.

Like most books of this nature, I have been urged by a group of good friends to get it out to the public (they called it my civic duty!) to mainly help the young and the young at heart who are entering the corporate world with rose-coloured glasses in the mistaken belief that the corporation will deliver them happiness by believing their mission statements and cultural mantras.

At the same time, I hope this work, or more importantly, its author, will not be viewed as someone who is bitter and angry with corporations. I just wish to use my experience and history to put the corporate role in one's life into perspective and relevance.

Good luck!

Acknowledgments

To my late Uncle Anton who taught me at a young age that beyond doubt 'education would be my greatest investment'. Uncle Anton was also ahead of his time by living by the modern concept of 'paying it forward'; when my dear uncle did business, whether selling companies or his own personal assets like motor vehicles, he would always sell a little below market value in order to leave enough profit for the next person to achieve their goals.

To my mum and dad who left the ravaged and torn country of Malta after WWII and made their way to the wonderful suburbs of Sydney, Australia, to raise a family, and where my brother and sister are still a close family unit with good family values. Our parents also taught us about equality and fairness, and introduced us to great European food. I will be forever grateful for being the son of European immigrants growing up in the western suburbs of Sydney.

Rex Bills, who I have known since the age of three where we grew up in 'Toongabbie Heights', has taught me more about street smarts and on how to deal with people than any MBA professor or textbook ever could.

To the unknown person down at Fairy Bower, Manly, who no matter what type of weather we were having always went in for a dip at the pool and greeted passers-by with a smile and the wonderful ditty of 'Your health is your wealth'.

Finally, to my wife and best friend, who has over the decades provided me with the spiritual light I (being an egotistical, rational thinker) was so sadly lacking in my life. She shares with me her joy, gives me inspiration and feeds my soul every day.

About the author

Mark Camilleri has over 27 years' industry experience in the information technology sector, particularly with start-ups and companies facing sales difficulties. Globally established and multi resident in Australia, UK and the USA; companies included Managing Director roles at Onyx Software and Siebel Systems, and Director of Customer Relationship Management (CRM) Asia Pacific at SPL WorldGroup. In these roles, Mark has been responsible for achieving multi-million-dollar sales and year on year quantum growth. Other industry roles include three years with Oracle Systems where he established the Australian/New Zealand Enterprise Resource Planning (ERP) sales teams, and three years at Dun & Bradstreet as Business Development Manager.

Often controversial and passionate about customer service, Mark is widely acknowledged as one of Australia's leading CRM authorities. He is an astute strategist, renowned for his exemplary skills in opening new markets, establishing go- to-market models, and aligning the sales strategies to exceed customer and corporate expectations.

Mark has been a keynote speaker on the issues and drivers impacting businesses today and a frequent presenter at industry events in the Asia Pacific region. Additionally, his views on customer management and its impact on business are frequently requested by the media.

He holds an MBA in Finance & Accounting and Bachelor of Business Law & Accounting.

Mark now retired currently resides with his wife Vicki and family in mountains of Queenstown New Zealand.

Printed in Great Britain
by Amazon